I0201780

THE
DISPENSATION
OF
THE LION &THE
LAMB

H.A.LEWIS

The Dispensation of the Lion and the Lamb

ISBN: 978-0-9904360-6-5 Soft cover

This book was printed in the United States of America.

The wonderful imagery of the lion and the lamb imagery was designed by Joanna Bobst who resides in Switzerland

Thank you so much for your labor of love

TABLE OF CONTENTS

Introduction 6

Chapter 1 9
A Man Sent By God

Chapter 2 17
King of Kings

Chapter 3 27
Warning to the Churches of Today

Chapter 4 49
The Three-Strand Cord of the Lamb

Chapter 5 63
Final Acts of the Lamb

Chapter 6 73
Favorite Images of Christ

Chapter 7 77
The Infant in the Manger

Chapter 8   79
  The Young Jesus

Chapter 9   81
  Jesus' Baptism

Chapter 10   83
  The Young Rabbi

Chapter 11   87
  The Lamb on the Donkey

Chapter 12   87
  The Beaten Lamb

Chapter 13   101
  The Resurrected Lamb

Chapter 14   103
  Behold the Lion of the Tribe of Judah

Chapter 15   129
  God is a God of Love

Introduction

I was almost thirteen years of age when I saw my very first lamb. Looking at that little woolly animal, I couldn't remember ever seeing something so cute and so gentle.

The other children around me were touching and petting it. They were cheerfully exclaiming how cute and cuddly the little creature was. However, I was afraid to touch it because it looked so fragile, and I did not want to hurt it in any way.

I recall wondering how anyone could want to hurt anything so soft and gentle, which differed greatly to my life so full of pain and suffering. As I gazed at the sweet gentle-natured lamb I momentarily forgot how horrifying the pain in my life was. Sadly it would remain that way for many years to come until another Lamb would enter my life.

The same day I met this other Lamb was the same day I found that He was also portrayed as another creature entirely different from the gentle lamb. This other animal is anything but gentle.

When a little lamb opens its mouth and bleats, anyone around him will laugh at how cute he is and immediately reach out to him. Comparatively when this other creature opens his mouth people will instinctively run and hide or breathe a sigh of relief that he is confined to a cage. When the lion, the mighty king of the beasts roars everything within the sound of his voice will tremble. There is absolutely no gentleness in the sound of a lion's roar as there is in the bleating of the lamb. Though there is such a stark contrast between a lion and a lamb, their distinctions would play a big part in my life years later.

It is extraordinary that both the gentle lamb and the mighty lion are characteristics of the same being. In one instance He is the Lamb of God who took away my sins. Moreover, He is, in the very same instance, a Lion of Judah who stood in defense of me against my enemies.

The Lamb of God! The Lion of Judah! The Son of God!

Two halves making one whole! It is within Jesus Christ, the living Son of God that we find both distinct characteristics. He is not only my personal Savior, but He is also my Deliverer. Welcome to the double nature of the Son of God!

The International Publishing team of H.A.Lewis Ministries

CHAPTER ONE

••••••••••••••••••••••••••••••

A Man Sent By God

In *John 1:28, 29* we read where John the Baptist is at Bethabara (Bethany) beyond the Jordan baptizing. Why was he doing this? To better understand John's purpose we must refer back to *John 1:6-9*. We read that there was a man sent by God or from God whose name was John. He was to be the witness and to bear the witness of the Light, that through Him all might believe. This was the true Light, which gives light to every man coming into the world.

According to *John 1:10, 11* Jesus, the Light, was in the world, and the world was made by Him, and the world didn't know Him. He came to His own and His own did not receive Him.

During this time the priests and the Levites were sent by the Jewish people to ask John who he was and by what authority did he baptize. John told them he was not the Christ, and neither was he Elijah nor the Prophet. John simply stated that he was a voice of one crying in the wilderness. He was to make straight the way of the Lord as the prophet Isaiah said.

These same religious people of the day then challenged John again. Since he claimed he wasn't Christ or Elijah, or the Prophet, they wanted to know by what authority or right did he baptize. In response John told them he baptized with water but there was coming someone after him whose sandals he was not worthy to untie. This someone would baptize them with the spirit and fire.

The very next day Jesus comes to John to be baptized in order to fulfill all righteousness. It is here that John introduces Jesus as the Lamb of God who takes away the sins of the world. It is John's introduction which acquaints us with the sweet gentle nature of Jesus.

In nature lambs are soft, gentle, and very sweet natured. No matter what happens they do not react in anger or violence. They prefer to avoid trouble and conflict at all costs. Those who have a lamb-like nature do not fight wars nor do they join street gangs to terrorize neighborhoods. They will give all they have, even their own lives without protest or strife.

Let's look at this side of Jesus' personality very closely. It is very important we understand why the Lamb had to come first. When we understand this, we will understand the very merciful nature of God the Father.

The Birth of the Lamb

....

The birth date of Jesus is **not** December 25th, as so many people believe. This date was actually the day that the son of Nimrod and Semiramis was born. The birth date of the Son of God, Jesus Christ was more than likely sometime in the spring.

In nature this is when all ewes gave birth to lambs. Unlike humans there is only one season in which ewes give birth and that is in the month of Nissan or Nisan, which is the spiritual new year of the Jews. Furthermore, there is only one reason why shepherds would be in the fields watching their flocks, even at night. It was the birthing season for the lamb.

Comparing the birthing season of the lambs to Christ's birth, there are some interesting facts to consider. The Lamb, Christ, was born in a cave and laid in a manger or feeding trough for animals. This cave was used as a place for animals to give birth. And the first visitors to bear witness to the birth of the Lamb of God were shepherds who were watching over their flocks as their ewes were pregnant and ready to give birth to little lambs.

Around Bethlehem the birth of special lambs took place as well. These special lambs would be set aside as the Passover lamb. Passover lambs were to be one year old and without spot or blemish. According to Passover law the lamb had to be born on the 10th of Nisan. A year later they would be brought in and kept for four days in the home and on the 14th day of

Nisan, which was Passover, they became a blood sacrifice.

The original Passover can be found in *Exodus 12:3-14*. God commanded the Israelites that on the 10th of Nisan every man was to take a lamb for his family, and they were to keep it until the 14th of the month where the whole assembly of the congregation of Israel would kill it at twilight. They were to apply the blood on the doorposts and lintel and the death angel would pass over the homes where the blood was applied.

According to the rabbinic law Christ, would have had to have been born on the 10th of Nisan and crucified on the 14th of Nisan as the Passover lamb was.

To accurately fulfill the Feast of Passover, His birth fulfilled all the necessities of the birth of the Passover lamb just as His death on the 14th of Nisan at twilight as the lambs were being sacrificed fulfilled the time of sacrifice. Moreover, his resurrection three days later on the *17th of Nisan*, fulfilled the feast of first fruits.

Next we see Jesus as a young boy sitting in the temple with the teachers both listening and answering them concerning the faith. As we follow Him in His young life we find a gentle caring young man who brings blessings everywhere He goes. Even during His famous forty-day fast in the desert we don't see an angry response to the devil's temptations. Instead, we see a man whose confidence is in His Father and His words. Without screaming or threatening He calmly uses the scriptures to rebuke and repel the enemy. *(Luke 4:1-13)*

In *Matthew 4:23-24* we see the personality and nature of the lamb being manifested as Jesus went from village to village doing good. As He met different people, it did not matter what kind of people they were or what they suffered from, Jesus stopped and took personal time to directly communicate with them and then taught them how they were to live in God's kingdom. Everyone who came to Him was not turned away. All were treated equally from the youngest to the oldest.

Throughout Jesus' time here on the earth, the lamb's nature was constantly evident in everything He did. However, the only time the image of the lion manifested during the incarnation of Jesus was when He dealt with devils or hypocrites.

It is when Jesus sees the disrespect of His Father's house in *Matthew 21: 12, 13* and in *John 2:13-16* that we see the nature of the lion. With a scourge of small cords He drives the moneychangers out of the temple. Unlike the lamb nature, the lion nature lasted for only a short period because soon afterward He is gently teaching those listening and healing the sick.

Imagine the surprise of the people when this gentle Lamb of God opened His mouth and the roar of the Lion of Judah came forth from Him!

It is extremely important for us to understand that Jesus exhibited the lamb nature, not because he had to be but because he chose to be. Absolutely everything about the first coming of Christ was done by choice.

**God chose to send His Son as
the sacrificial lamb**

....

The Son **chose** to come as a sin
offering. His sacrifice would take
away the sins of the whole world and
restore to the Father what He lost.
His sacrifice would also restore to
man what he gave away by **choice**.

CHAPTER TWO

······················

King of Kings

The King of all kings was born in a cave and wrapped in rags. This fact alone is completely astounding. Imagine it! He, who created all of creation, who owned all the gold and silver and every precious stone not only on the earth, but also on every planet in every universe and galaxy in all of creation, would choose to be born in a manger to poor parents. The swaddling cloth He was wrapped in was not purple or the fine linen of the earthly kings or the wealthy.

The first time I traveled to Egypt and Nigeria, I witnessed the great poverty both of these countries had. After seeing the immense poverty everywhere I was truly thankful for what I had back home in America. As I reminisce of those times I traveled to these two countries, I wonder what was on the mind of Jesus when He looked at the earthly Jerusalem and the poverty of mankind compared to His heavenly home and the beauty of the New Jerusalem being built there.

Many times we grumble at what we temporarily give up for the sake of the gospel. Yet without complaint the Lamb of God gave up willingly the wealth of His kingdom, which was rightfully His, for our sake. It would still be absolutely amazing if He did this for us if we were His friends; however, we were His enemies and far away from Him and His Father. How utterly marvelous! It is beyond our understanding why He has done this for all mankind.

It is simply the nature of the lamb to be compassionate. It did not matter to the Lord how we preceded Him. He came to be a sin offering to return man back to His Father. All that matters to Him was that His Father's will was accomplished and fulfilled. As is the nature of the lamb, He would choose not to run or resist. Neither would he fight.

If He had decided to demonstrate the nature of the lion, things would have been greatly different. It is not in a lion's nature to submit. Jesus would not have been taken without a fight, and He would never have been a willing sacrifice.

I particularly love the story of Aslan the Lion in the Chronicles of Narnia written by C.S. Lewis. In his story, Aslan goes willingly to be sacrificed at the hands of the witch.

Unlike Aslan, the Lion of Judah will not go to be sacrificed at the hands of his enemies. Instead, when his dispensation comes, he will destroy all of his enemies and ours.

It is true the enemy may try to imitate the Lion of Judah. Nevertheless he destroys and devours all that he can. The truth of the matter is he is only an imitation, a counterfeit of the real thing. He is a jackal that seeks to be a lion and never will be. When the true Lion comes the enemy's reign of terror will come to an eternal end for all times.

It is amazing the love and compassion the Lord God has for His creation called man. When we read the story of how all things came into existence, we see that of all of God's creation except for one came into reality by the spoken word.

God spoke the earth, the solar system, the waters, the birds, the fish, the cattle, and all of the animals into existence. In the creation of man he formed him from the dust of the earth; from the very soil of the planet he was meant to rule over and not to be ruled by.

God gave man a physical body which was needed to rule and live in the physical world. Yet more important than this God breathed His own breath (spirit) into man. This gave man not only physical life and earthly citizenship, but it also gave him spiritual life so he could also have the right to be a spiritual citizen of the kingdom of his Father God (*Genesis 2:7*)

God took a personal interest in the creation of man. He made all other aspects of creation in the image He desired. However, man was formed differently. God formed man in His very image. God is a triune being: Father, Son and Holy Spirit.

Man was created a triune being: spirit, soul and body. No other creation was created in this way, only man.

Man was also created with something no other of God's creation possessed and that was the right to choose to obey and to disobey. Man, in all honesty, was the only creation who could choose to disobey by free will. He was the only one who could sin by choice and sadly that is what he chose to do. Man's free will to disobey is how sin came into this world, which was created perfect by God.

It was just one act of disobedience by Adam and the ownership of this world was transferred from Adam, who was meant to be the rightful ruler of the earth – a son of God, to Satan, a thief and murderer – the enemy of God. Many times I have pondered how great a price was paid because of disobedience giving birth to sin. Then I am reminded of how great a price was paid to deliver us from sin and to restore us back to God.

It really is extraordinary to fully grasp the fact that only the Lamb could pay the required price of redemption. The Lion, in all of its great strength, could not. Only the Lamb in its meekness could. Imagine the devil's amazement when his great powers and his three associates found themselves completely overcome and their powers destroyed forever.

Can you see the expression on the faces of Death, Hell, and the Grave, when the gates were thrown open wide and the Lamb of God, who they thought they had destroyed for good, walks in their midst? One moment they are celebrating how they defeated Him, and in the next moment He walks right up to them and takes their keys and authority away from them forever.

It really should not have been too much of a surprise. After all, this was the same Lamb who gave the keys of the kingdom and all authority over the enemy and his kingdom (*Matthew 16:16-19*) to all of his followers.

The Lamb was meek. He was humble. He was obedient in all things to His Father. He was gentle and compassionate; however, He was no push over. This Lamb could roar with the power of a Lion if He had to. Even though he had great strength, He refrained from using it unwisely.

It took a considerable amount of inner strength to submit Himself to the will of His Father. What was it like for the Lord to be walking among His creation and they did not know Him? He came in physical contact with those He originally gave life to, and from their ancestors He had a chosen people whom he guided night and day through the desert, making sure there was no sick among them.

During their time in the desert He caused their clothes and sandals not to wear out. He provided food and water and gave them the Law so they could be guided spiritually by the commandments as He guided them physically through the desert for forty years.

This Lamb who walked among them was the same one who delivered them from slavery and showed His power by destroying the fake gods of Egypt. He parted the Red Sea, allowing them to all cross over safely and then drowned their enemies. (*Exodus 14:28*)

Here they were, doing their daily ritual of offering up prayers and praises and incense and sacrifices to God, yet unaware that Immanuel God in the flesh, the very one they were looking for, was walking among them.

Just as He did in the forty years they spent wandering in the desert, He was performing the same miracles among them now. He was healing the sick, providing food, and giving freedom to those who sought after them. Still, they did not know Him.

What was it like when the very Word of God stood in the temple reading from the scroll the very words He commanded Moses and the prophets, and King David to write? It is the gentle nature of the Lamb displayed as He referred worship and directed all praise to His Father. He understood perfectly that He came not to draw attention to Himself but to point the way to the Father.

Truly, this Lamb was the King of kings and sat on the eternal throne as God; in spite of the fact that he was born in a cave and laid in a manger where animals ate because there was no room in the inn.

Now, that He was right here with them and watched them with eyes of love, there sadly seemed to be no room in their hearts for Him, just as there was no room in the inn for Him at birth.

Though the mountains be shaken and the hills be removed, yet my unfailing love for you will not be shaken nor my covenant of peace be removed," says the LORD, who has compassion on you. Isaiah 54:10

CHAPTER THREE

••••••••••••••••••••••••••••••

Warning to the Churches of Today

I give a warning to the churches of today. Learn a lesson from the religious people during the time of Christ, the dispensation of the Lamb, when He walked among His own people. I am not referring to the pagan religions but those who proclaimed to be the chosen people of God.

Isn't it strange that three Magi kings from the Orient followed a star to seek after the one born the King of the Jews? They discerned the signs; yet those who grew up with the Law and the promise of the coming of the Messiah did not recognize the signs of His birth.

For the next thirty plus years, except for a brief time when He was very young and His foster father brought Him to Egypt to keep Him safe from Herod *(Matthew 2:13)*, He would live among them having His life observed by all.

God told the prophet, Simeon, that he would not die before he saw the fulfillment of the promise of the coming of the Messiah. When the Lamb was an infant, Simeon held Him in his aged hands and proclaimed that he could go to his rest because he had seen the promise of the Messiah come to pass. (*Luke 2:25-33*) Likewise the prophetess, Anna, an aged mother of Israel who lived in the temple, spoke to everyone who was seeking redemption about this child. (*Luke 2:36-38*)

Despite all the signs, the vast majority of the religious leaders of the day, the Pharisees, the Sadducees, the scribes, and lawyers who spent hours in studying the Law, were blind to the fact that the Promised One was among them. All of their knowledge of the Law and the Word, all of their religious observances and their sacrifices, and all of their religious duties did nothing to open their eyes spiritually so they could see.

How could it be that all these religious leaders could not see what one elderly prophet and prophetess, three pagan kings and several lowly shepherds could plainly see? The answer is simple. Religion blinds the eyes of men to God's truth, but those who seek relationship with the Lamb will have their eyes opened every time to His truth.

Can you imagine what must have crossed His mind when the people, the priests, and the religious leaders did not believe in Him, but also His own immediate family? I am sure Mary must have told His four brothers, James, Joses, Juda and Simon, and even His sisters about their older brother's birth. They did not believe He was the Promised One until after His resurrection. (*Mark 6:3*)

How many times was the heart of this gentle Lamb broken? Did He draw away from everyone to ask the Father for more grace to continue doing the Father's will? When spending those long hours alone with His Father did He ask for more strength to continue, as you and I would have? No one knows but the Father and Him what was said.

Look at His heart when He stood at the tomb of Lazarus and groaned in His spirit and then wept in *John 11:35* because of their lack of faith. After everything He had done and all the miracles, there were still those close to Him and whom He considered friends that lacked faith and understanding of who He was. In spite of all this the nature of the Lamb was in charge, and He was moved with compassion for their sake and to confirm what He stated that He was the resurrection and life. He called Lazarus forth from the grave.

This miracle, instead of convincing the religious leaders that He was the chosen one, the greater Son of David who would one day sit on the throne of David forever, upset and worried them instead. This Lamb was the Messiah they had been waiting so long for. He was the answer to their prayers. Instead of allowing their eyes to be opened spiritually, they chose to close their hearts to Him so their religious empire would not be touched.

Not only did they seek to kill the Lamb, but they also planned to take the life of Lazarus so the common people would not continue to believe in Jesus because of the miracle of Lazarus being raised from the dead. Regardless of how unbelievably heartless the religious leaders were, Jesus continued to do merciful acts of compassion to show how much He cared for the people. He was fulfilling all of the Messianic prophecies of His first coming and they were blind to it.

The heart of this great Lamb of God must have been repeatedly broken from the reaction of those who, bound by religion, refused to open their eyes and ears to truth, and their hearts to Him. It is amazing to imagine the Lamb going from village to village, doing what the God of Israel commanded and teaching the very Law that these religious leaders taught and proclaimed as loudly as possible that they believed in. Moreover these religious leaders taught the common people that they were to hear and obey the Law, yet they did not keep the Law themselves.

Recently I had the privilege to go to Israel. It was a dream come true for me because I have always wanted to walk where my Savior walked. I don't know what I was really expecting to see when I got there, but it truly was not what I thought it would be. At every historical place where something of importance in the life of Jesus occurred, there were souvenir shops, restaurants, and all kinds of monetary actions going on.

When we went down to the Jordan River to baptize a young woman, we were stopped and told that since we were not a part of a tour group and had not made a reservation we would not be allowed in. It was only when I told the curator that I was a Jewish rabbi, and it was my right to be there as a son of Abraham and since he wasn't Jewish he had no authority to stop me, that he reluctantly let us pass to go to the river.

As we got to the river he walked towards us and said we had to rent a white gown and towel from them because the clothes we brought with us was not acceptable. To avoid a scene, we paid to rent the gown and towel. While getting ready for the baptism I wondered: what would John the Baptist have done or even what Jesus would have done in this situation? As for John the Baptist, I truly don't know how he would have responded, whereas Jesus would have fulfilled all righteousness and rendered unto Caesar what was Caesar's.

Finally, standing on a hill looking over Jerusalem, seeing the greed of the money changers, the lack of respect for the historical site, blind religious leaders, the Jews, the Moslems, and the so called Christian church, all I could do was follow the example of Jesus and wept over Jerusalem. As I stood there with a broken heart, I could hear the voice of the Lamb as He cried so many years ago.

And when He was come near, He beheld the city, and wept over it, saying, if thou hardest known, even thou, at least in this thy day, the things which belong unto thy peace! But now they are hid from thine eyes. For the days shall come upon thee, that thine enemies shall cast a trench about thee, and compass thee round, and keep thee in on every side, and shall lay thee even with the ground, and thy children within thee; and they shall not leave in thee

one stone upon another; because thou knewest not the time of thy visitation.
[Luke 19:41-44]

....

I truly wonder with all my heart if the Church today will be so busy being religious that when He comes again we will, like the Jews of old, miss Him this time as well. Oh my! Lord forbid this should happen!

I am in awe at the gentleness of the Lamb. He had all the power there was in the universe. In fact, with a word He brought all of creation into being. He could have easily spoken one word and destroyed everything; instead, He chose to continue to be gentle and bless those who were rejecting Him.

As a child I remember this man in the projects where I grew up. He was an extremely big man; however, he was very gentle and patient. A lot of the older guys tried to get a reputation by beating this man in a fight. No matter what they did He would not get angry and fight.

One day three older kids were working on a car. They had it up on a jack and one of them was under the car working on it. All of a sudden the jack fell and the car came crashing down and the young man was trapped under it. The other young men tried in vain to get their friend out. The news of what happened went all around the project. People came from everywhere to see what had happened. Nobody knew what to do and help was a long way off. 911 didn't exist back then.

The car, which had fallen, was a 1957 Plymouth and weighed a lot more than cars do today. The father and mother of the kid trapped underneath came rushing to the scene of the accident. When the father saw the car on top of his son, he was devastated and felt completely helpless.

What happened next I will never forget. Out of nowhere came this gentle giant of a man that the guys had teased, insulted, and repeatedly challenged to fight. As he walked through the crowd, the people just stared at him, wondering why he was there. Some people said he came to see what had happened to one of his adversaries, perhaps even to privately gloat over what had happened.

Instead he very quietly walked through the crowd, ignored their gossip, bent down and grabbed the front bumper of the Plymouth. Standing up he lifted the front end of the car up to the level of his chest. As he held the car up several of the men in the crowd grabbed the young man and pulled him to safety.

Once the young man was pulled free he lowered the car and this gentle giant simply turned and walked away, not even waiting to be thanked. As silently as he came, he left. I will tell you this, after seeing the man's strength, nobody dared ever to challenge or tease him again. Now everyone in the project realized that the man did not fight because he was afraid or that he couldn't. He didn't fight because he chose not to.

This is how I see the Lamb. It wasn't that He couldn't get angry. It was that He chose not to get angry and to bless instead.

There is a religion today which teaches that because Christ was crucified for our sake He is angry with us and we cannot approach Him except through His mother, the Virgin Mary.

This is a terrible lie. Remember the word of the Lamb as He cried *in Matthew 11:28*, "come unto me all ye that labor and are heavy laden and I will give you rest." The way to the Lamb of God is open to all men who are willing to hear His voice and come to Him. We don't need anyone to intercede to Him for us because the scripture tells us that He lives to always intercede for us to the Father, for the Lamb who was sacrificed for us is now the eternal High Priest who lives to intercede for us to His heavenly Father.

Let us pause for a moment and imagine what it must have been like for the Lamb, on the remaining night and day of His physical life as the Lamb of God who was sent to destroy the power of sin over man. He came to defeat the adversary and to take away the authority of Death, Hell and the Grave. It is absolutely astounding that

God would send a Lamb to face the five most powerful enemies of man.

Wait! Did you realize I named only four instead of five? He came to defeat the Adversary, Death, Hell, and the Grave. According to my calculations, this only makes four. However, I want to look first at our spiritual enemies, which the Lamb defeated in the three nights and days He was in the bowels of the earth.

Then we will look at our emotional and physical enemies, which is found in 1 *John 2:16*: the lust of the eyes, the pride of life, and the lust of the flesh. It is truly the power of sin over the creation of God. It's exactly the way God said in His word, "As the heavens are way above the earth so are My ways higher than man and My thoughts above your thoughts." (*Isaiah 55:9*)

Can you imagine the look of surprise and horror on the face of the adversary when the Lord Jesus in the form of the Lamb stood in front of the gates of hell and cried with a loud voice, "Open wide ye gates so the King of Glory may come in"? (*Psalm*

24:7-10) We can see the fulfillment of the scripture in Matthew 16:18 that on the rock of faith the church of Christ will be built and the gates of hell shall not prevail against it.

Can you just imagine what was going through the mind of Satan as he beheld the One who had just been spit on by the religious leaders of His people and denied by one of His own disciples who swore he would never deny Him? What were His thoughts as another disciple betrayed Him and delivered Him into the hands of His enemies? From the kiss of betrayal, He was brought to the leader of the Gentiles to be beaten, mocked, have a crown of thorns forced down on his forehead with thorns averaging 3-6 inches in length. The crown was pushed so hard onto His head the long thorns could easily pierce through His cranium. Then He was beaten 39 times with a cat-o-nine tails that had stones, bones, and other sharp objects attached to the nine cords forming the whip.

The beating wasn't entrusted to just any soldier. It had to be the strongest and the most experienced soldier in the art of torment. In fact, the beating Jesus received was so terrible; many victims of the cat-o-nine tails had simply died from the harshness of it alone. After the beating He was forced to carry the final instrument of His torture across His shoulders and back, which was torn open and shredded so the very muscles were exposed.

Finally He was nailed to the cross through the wrists, which were considered part of the hand, and right through the most painful nerve in the whole body, sending incredible burning through the arms and shoulders.

The pressure on the lungs was tremendous. Air could come in but could not go out, causing the lungs to fill and expand. This in turn caused the blood to thicken which forced the heart to strain to pump the blood. Eventually this would lead to congestive heart failure causing the victim to die of a broken heart literally.

After seeing all this then the watching soldiers proclaimed Jesus dead and took Him down from the cross. Satan truly believed he finally won the battle that the promised seed of the woman who was supposed to crush his head laid dead and could never cause him any more trouble or defeat in any way whatsoever as he watched them prepare Him for His burial. (*Genesis 3:19*)

It seemed Satan had a short-term memory problem for he forgot who lay wrapped in clothes in the grave, the very author of all creation. Satan may not have been standing right by His side but he was close enough to see Him speak all of creation into being. How could Satan believe he had caused the death of the author of life?

Pride truly blinds a person to the truth. As previously mentioned you can only imagine the look of horror and surprise on Satan's face when he looked in the face of the Promised One, the seed of the woman who would not only bruise his head but defeat him along with his companions death, hell, and the grave. Soon mankind would never need to fear him ever again.

What I believe shocked him the most was that Jesus' face was not the face of the warrior Messiah, the lion. Instead, it was the face of the Savior of mankind, the image of the loving gentle face of the lamb. However, I would imagine the image of the warrior, the Lion of the tribe of Judah was superimposed over the face of the sacrificed Lamb. This dual-natured King would sit on the throne of His father David forever, the greater Son of David, the King of Israel.

Perhaps when Satan looked into the eyes of his Creator, he saw a hint of compassion in those eyes of mercy. As scripture said, "God isn't willing that any man should perish but all come to the knowledge of Jesus as Lord." I know this scripture pertains to mankind but I know it hurts the Lord to lose any of His creation.

Just as Adam was tested as to where his loyalty lay and how obedient he would be to the command of God, so also were the angels tested to see where their loyalties lay as well. The only difference is man was not in the presence of God continually as the angels were. Neither was man present when God spoke creation into being.

We don't know how long Satan and the angels were with God in heaven, what they saw and the blessings they received. However, we do know that the fall of Satan and those who followed him in rebellion occurred before the creation of Adam because Satan was already a rebel against God.

At the very beginning of Creation Satan was already trying to hurt God by destroying it. Many wonder if Satan and his fallen angels would repent, would God forgive them? After all man has rebelled against God and has sinned over and over again. Yet if he truly repents and asks God for forgiveness God is more than willing to forgive. The difference is man was created on earth and had not been in heaven to see God face to face and the wonders of His acts of creation.

Satan and the angels who fell were created in heaven and had the honor of beholding God in all of His splendor and to see His awesome power demonstrated in creation. Another difference is Satan and his legion of fallen angels tempts man constantly, but there was no one to tempt Satan to rebel. It was his pride and arrogance.

Satan has no one but himself to blame for his fall. I am sure if Satan had seen that something was wrong in him, which was causing him to act in a very destructive way, and he had asked God for help, the Lord would have gladly done it. Therefore, I am sorry but there is simply no sympathy for the devil as the famous rock stars ask for in their songs.

In the uncanonized book of *Enoch 13:4*, the fallen angels, under the leadership of Azazel, petitions Enoch to ask God for forgiveness for themselves and their offspring. When Enoch approached God on their behalf, he was told the fallen angels would never be forgiven and all of their offspring, the giants that were in the earth, would be destroyed.

Forgiveness from sin is our privilege not a right. It was freely given to mankind and should be taken advantage of by man. We must understand that the Spirit of God will not always strive with man. This dispensation of grace will come to an end and then will come judgment.

I believe that the end of the dispensation of the Lamb is the ending of the age of grace which will usher in the age of judgment, the dispensation of the Lion, not the merciful Savior but the righteous judge. The Jesus of this dispensation of the Lion is vastly different than the Jesus of the Lamb, the merciful Savior. In fact John, the beloved disciple who laid his head on the Lamb of God's chest, did not immediately recognize Him in His manifestation of the judge of the living and dead. He tells us in *Revelation 1:13-17* that the image of Jesus which he saw in this vision was unlike anything he had seen Jesus as in the past.

In this image John said that the Lord's garment went all the way to His feet and was tied with a girdle of gold indicating His divinity, not humanity. Then John said

His hair and head were pure white as wool and snow, which indicates that the Lord is holy and pure. His eyes were like a flame of fire and his feet as fine brass, showing He was standing in righteous judgment. His voice was as the sound of many waters, showing the power and authority of His word. The description John the Beloved gives is not the portrait of the Lamb of God. It is picture of the magnificent Lion of the tribe of Judah, the righteous judge of all.

Can you imagine what John thought when he finally grasped that this divine righteous judge which stood before him was the same Jesus who as the Lamb of God walked with him on the earth? This righteous judge was the same Jesus who was crucified before his eyes and buried then resurrected. It was the same Jesus that he and the other disciples witnessed ascending on high with the promise of His return. Although he was the same Jesus John knew so well, He was not the gentle Lamb of God who came to take away the sins of the world. This was not the compassionate Messiah who had already suffered and died for the lost and paid the price to restore man back to fellowship with the Father.

No, this was a very different side of the Jesus John once knew and walked with. This persona was so different from the gentle Lamb that John had to be introduced to this manifestation of his Lord. This was the warrior King and the Messiah which was prophesied to come and what the Jewish nation was waiting for. This was the Messiah who would deliver and redeem the nation of Israel and who would judge the Gentile nations of the world.

This was the greater Son of David who would sit on His Father's throne and rule the nation of Israel and the Gentile nations from the city of David, Jerusalem, the capital of the whole world. This was the One that Jerusalem and all of Israel had waited for so long. It's just they couldn't see or understand that the Lamb had to come first to restore man back to God before the Lion came to judge the nation. For if God's divine order had not occurred, there simply would not have been any reason for the Lamb to come because mankind would have been judged and condemned. Moreover, Israel would never be restored because it would never have been given the chance to accept the One they had rejected.

CHAPTER FOUR

....

The Three -Strand Cord of the Lamb

The Lamb of God is gentle, kind,
loving and more than willing to forgive
anyone who truly repents. The love of God
is beyond our ability to understand.
Scripture teaches us that even before the
foundation of the world was made, God had
already put a plan together to restore
mankind back to Him.

It is beyond my ability to fully
comprehend the amazing love of God for
man. When two men are enemies they do
not bless their adversary; instead, they do all
in their power to destroy them and any that
would side with them. It does not matter
whether they are right or wrong. Yet God,
who is righteous and holy and is the only
one with absolute right to condemn and
destroy His enemies, does all in His power
to bless them. Scripture teaches us that while
we were a far off and enemies of God, He
loved us and sent His Son to die for us.

It only shows that if the Father is merciful, compassionate, and forgiving then the Son of God would have the same attributes as His Father. It also shows that we will also develop these exact same virtues of the one I call Lord.

Today there is a big movement of people proclaiming to have the office of prophet or apostle; although, some may have gifts like prophecy and tongues with interpretation, they sadly do not exhibit the fruits of the Spirit. It is not by the gifts of the Spirit that we show maturity of our spirit. Instead the maturity of our spirit is shown by whether or not we have the fruits of the Spirit of God.

When a person has both the gifts and the fruits of the Spirit active in their life, their ministry will produce signs, wonders and miracles. The kingdom of God will expand while the kingdom of the adversary will fall, and the name of God will be exalted and highly lifted up.

Jesus is the example of what we should be and what we should do. Although

He was the Son of God, He learned obedience through the things He suffered. (*Hebrews 5:8*) We know Jesus was the Son of God. However, to be fair to us, Jesus learned the same way we do by the things we suffer through, by learning from one another and by studying the word of God.

The fullness of God's Spirit and the gifts of the Holy Spirit were manifested in the life of Jesus and He knew all things because of His great discernment. He had both the gift of prophecy and the office of the prophet. Jesus also manifested the different gifts of healing. Whether it was a fever as in Peter's mother-in-law or leprosy as in the case of the ten lepers, He healed them. Jesus was empowered to meet their special need.

He had the ability to raise the dead as in the case of the only son of a widow woman who was on the way to be buried (*Luke 7:12-15*), as in the case of Jarius' daughter who was dead (*Luke 9:51-56*), and as in the most famous case of Lazarus (*John 11:43-44*).

Jesus had the gift of miracles, which we see when He took the loaves and fishes and fed the multitude. He had the power over demons. With just a word He could set a person free as in the case of the demoniac possessed by Legion and Mary Magdalene, who was possessed with seven demons.

The fullness of the Spirit of God was manifested in Him at His water baptism where the Holy Spirit descended on Him like a dove and His Father proclaimed Him as His Son whom He was well pleased with. Immediately after this wonderful endorsement, Jesus was led into the desert to be tested. It was not that the Father had any doubt in Jesus' faith or His willingness to obey or that Jesus doubted who He was. No, it was to show the devil and the world whose He was, the one and only begotten Son of the Father.

Jesus knew not to take things into His own hands and try to do it in His own time. Even when His mother tried to get Him to do a miracle at the wedding in Canaan (Cana) (*John 2:1-5*), He replied to her request by addressing her as woman and stating my time has not yet come. This didn't mean He was not able to do miracles or start His ministry. As a Jewish male He knew that to try to start a ministry before He was thirty years of age would be useless because according to tradition you were not mature enough to be taken seriously until you were thirty years old.

Too many of us today would have rejected this concept and would have started our ministry when we wanted to; however, Jesus didn't come to do His own will. He came to do the will of the Father and to fulfill all of the law and customs so as not to blemish His calling in any way whatsoever. Look at Him in the temple at the age of twelve where His knowledge of the law and of scriptures was so profound it totally amazed the scribes and the doctors of the Law. (*Luke 2:46-47*) These were not the simple unlearned people; they were the religious experts of the day. Jesus was obedient in all things and knew to wait for the right time.

Jeremiah, the weeping prophet, when confronted by the Lord to begin the ministry he was created for, stated to the Lord that he was only a child and no one would listen to him. Jeremiah knew that before he was thirty, people wouldn't listen to his message. (*Jeremiah 1:4-7*)

The Lamb of God, although a Son of God, was willing to obey in all things so that His Father's will and not His own would be done. He chose not to take things into His own hands and rush to start His ministry.

I believe we can learn a valuable lesson from Him. It's true we are called to minister unto the Lord and for the Lord. We are filled with God's spirit; however, we must be willing to wait until the Lord tells us to go before we launch our ministry. If we wait on Him, then not only will we have the gifts of the Spirit but we also will have the maturity of the Spirit to handle the gifts and to fill one of the offices of the five ministries.

It is a good thing to say we have faith in God and that He will do what He promises; however, if we have faith, we must also have trust. Isn't having faith in

God the same as trusting Him? The answer is no. Faith means you believe God can do something He promised to do at the time He chooses to do so.

Do you recall God's promise to Abraham? He promised Abraham a son and Abraham had faith God could and would do what He promised. Of course this was pleasing in the sight of God, but how much more would God have been pleased if Abraham and Sarah would have trusted Him enough?

They didn't trust Him enough to let Him do it in His own time. Instead they tried to make it happen in their own way, which only ended in a problem that is still going on today between two half brothers Ishmael, the son of Hagar, the servant girl and Isaac, the son of Sarah, the free woman. (*Genesis 20:1-21*)

God promised David he would be king over all of Israel. David was a young man when Samuel anointed him king. God took twenty-five years to bring the promise to pass. Therefore, if God promised you a blessing have faith he will do it; more importantly trust Him to do it at the right time.

After all what is twenty-five years compared to eternity? Jesus had both great faith and complete trust in His Father. It was evident when He prayed at the tomb of Lazarus. "Father, I know You always hear Me when I pray, but for the sake of those people standing around Me I said it that they might believe Thou hath sent me." (*John 11:41-42*)

It is extremely important we grasp this truth. We believe God will answer our prayers, but do we trust that He always hears us? Faith and trust coming from the same person at the same time will result in the manifestation of the miraculous.

What was the powerful three-strand cord in the life of the Lamb of God which produced the victorious miracle working power in His life? They were faith, trust and obedience. With these three elements in our life, they will also produce the same manifestation of the power of God in our lives, so that the name of our God will be glorified and the kingdom of the adversary be destroyed and the kingdom of our Lord be expanded.

Many will use the excuse that Jesus' prayers were always answered because He was the Son of God. Remember this! If you are truly born again, then you too are a child of God and your prayers will always be heard. Jesus said to His disciples and all who follow Him that the works He did we would also do and greater things so that the Father would be glorified.

This is the main purpose of Christianity. Whatever we do, whether in word or deed, in the name of Jesus will bring glory to God. (*Colossians 3:15-17*) "Whatever you do in word or deed, do all in the name of the Lord Jesus, giving thanks to God the Father by Him."

When Jesus came in the dispensation of the Lamb, whatsoever He did in word or deed, He did it in thanks to His Father and to bring glory to God the Father. In *John 17:4*, Jesus says, "I have glorified Thee on the earth, I have finished the work which Thou hast given me to do."

The whole purpose of the Lamb was to redeem man back to God and to bring glory to His Father. He was obedient in everything He did, whether in word or deed. It was an act of extreme obedience in His death by crucifixion. He remained absolutely quiet through the mockery of a trial, which was illegally done at night. He remained silent during the testimony of false witnesses, even at the betrayal of a disciple and someone he befriended.

He continued His silence and displayed humility at the beating He received by the Roman soldiers, including the crucifixion. He only spoke on the way to the cross when He told the woman not to weep for Him but to weep for themselves and their children because of the days that were to come to the nation of Israel because of their rejection of their redeemer.

On the cross He expressed compassion and mercy to the thief who was crucified with Him and that His mother,

Mary, was going to be taken care of by His disciple, John, since His own siblings did not believe that Jesus was the Promised Messiah. (*Luke 23:42-43*; *John 19:26-27*)

The image of the Lamb was portrayed in the life, death, burial, resurrection and ascension of Jesus. The Lamb is seen again in heaven where in the book of Revelation, John weeps after being told there was no one worthy to open the book. One of the elders declares that the Lion of the tribe of Judah the root of David had prevailed to open the book and to loose the seven seals thereof. (*Revelation 5:5*)

John sees a Lamb standing as if slain having seven horns and seven eyes, which are the seven spirits of God sent forth through all the earth. This Lamb takes the book out of the right hand of Him who sits on the throne and the four and twenty elders and the four beasts who each having a harp and golden vial filled with odors, which are the prayers of the saints, begin to sing a new song to the Lamb of God. He was found to be worthy to open the book and open the seals for He, the Lamb, was slain and redeemed man from every tribe and nation, tongues and kindred by His blood. The Lamb had made men to be kings and priests unto God and they would reign on earth. (*Revelation 5:6-10*)

Afterwards, John sees and hears the voices of many angels round about the throne and the four beasts, twenty-four elders, and the number of angels was ten thousand times ten thousand and thousands of thousands proclaiming in a loud voice, "Worthy is the Lamb that was slain to receive power, and riches, and wisdom, and strength, and honor, and glory, and blessing." Every one above, which is in heaven, and the earth, and under the earth and such are in the sea and all that are in them saying, "blessings and glory, and power be unto Him who sits on the throne an unto the Lamb forever and ever." The four beasts say, "amen" and the four and twenty elders fall down again and worship Him who lives forever and ever. (*Revelation 5:11-14*)

All this takes place before what ushers in the final acts of the Lamb of God, before He is transformed into the Lion of the tribe of Judah, the root of David. Then John sees the Lamb of God who has seven horns and seven eyes, which represents the seven spirits of God who are sent forth through the whole world, begin to open one of the seals of the scroll of the judgment of God.

The one who was sent not to condemn the world but save it, (*John 3:17*), was now getting ready to judge the world.

For the Father judgeth no man for He hath committed all judgment to the Son. (*John 5:22*)

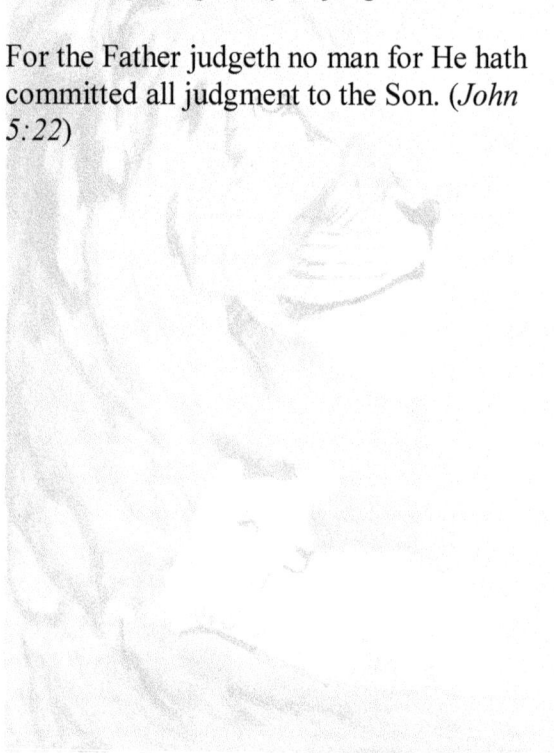

CHAPTER FIVE

••••••••••••••••••••••••••

Final Acts of the Lamb

In *Revelation 6* the Lamb begins opening the seven seals of the scroll. When the Lamb opens the first seal, the noise of thunder is heard and the white horse of the antichrist that is its rider is sent forth to conquer.

Next we see the Lamb opening the second seal and the red horse of war is let loose on the earth. A great sword was given to the rider of this horse and the power to take peace from the earth was his. Then the Lamb opens the third seal and the black horse of famine and poverty, and inflation come forth.

The fourth seal is opened and the pale horse is let loose, which is the horse of plague and her rider is Death, and Hell follows with him. Power is given unto them over the fourth part of the earth to kill with sword, with hunger, with death, and with the beasts of the earth.

Next we see the Lamb opening the fifth seal and we see the souls of the faithful who were slain for the Word of God, and for the testimony that they held. As the Lamb opens the sixth seal, there is a great earthquake and the sun becomes black as sackcloth made of hair, and the moon becomes as blood.

Then the stars of heaven fall unto the earth and the heaven departs as a scroll and every mountain and island are moved out of their places. This causes the kings of the earth and the great men and every man on the earth to fear and to hide themselves in the dens and the rocks of the mountains. Then all men cry out to the mountains and rocks to fall on them and to hide them from the face of Him who sits on the throne and from the wrath of the Lamb. For they now acknowledge that the great day of the wrath of the Lamb has come, and they know that no one will be able to stand against his great anger and righteous judgment.

Still under the opening of the sixth seal we see the sealing of the hundred and forty-four thousand witnesses, twelve thousand from each of the twelve tribes of Israel. Then we observe the great number of saints who have come out of the great tribulation having washed their robes in the blood of the Lamb making them white. These will never hunger or thirst anymore for the Lamb will provide all their needs and their tears will be wiped away by the One who sits on the throne.

Finally, the Lamb opens the seventh seal of the scroll, and there is complete silence in all of heaven for the space of half an hour. Then the seven angels, which stood before the throne of God, are given seven trumpets, and another angel comes and stands at the altar of God having a golden censer and he was given much incense to offer up with the prayers of the saints upon the golden altar before God.

Then the angel takes the censer and fills it with fire from the altar and casts it to the earth, and there are voices, thundering, lightning, and an earthquake. After this the seven angels with the seven trumpets prepare to get ready to sound their trumpets.

With each trumpet that sounds a part of the wrath of the Lamb is poured out. In the next seven advents, we must keep in mind that the Lord Jesus is still in His persona of the Lamb. He has not quite transformed into the Lion of the tribe of Judah.

It seems that the Lamb will handle the judgment of man's acts of rebellion against the kingdom of His Father, the One who sits on the throne. The Lamb takes care of the spiritual kingdom of heaven and the passing of righteous judgment of rebellious mankind. Afterward, I believe it is the Lord in His persona of the Lion of the tribe of Judah that defeats the rulers of the earth and establishes the physical kingdom of His Father on the face of the earth, where He will rule for a thousand years.

Pause a moment and consider the judgment of the Lamb of God and the attitude of men against this judgment. Jesus is still the Lamb for today. Though men are being judged for their rebellious acts, there is still an offer of redemption to any who will ask for it.

However the judgment of the Lamb, as the seven angels blow their trumpets at His leading, is vastly different than this dispensation of grace. The first angel sounds his trumpet and there falls hail and fire mingled with blood, and they are cast upon the earth, and a third part of the earth and trees are burned up and all the green grass is burned up.

Can you imagine the horror running through your mind if you are here when this first trumpet of the Lamb judgment sounds and you see the destruction of these trees and all of the green grass everywhere? You will literally be standing in a vast wasteland, yet man simply will not repent. In all that has already occurred on earth, man still refuses to obey God.

Then the second angel sounds and as it were a great mountain burning with fire is cast into the sea, and the third part of the sea becomes blood, and a third part of the creatures which were in the sea and had life. died, and a third part of the ships were destroyed.

The third angel sounds and there falls a great star from heaven, burning like a lamp and it falls upon a third of the rivers and upon the foundation of water. The name of this fallen star is Wormwood and a third part of the waters become wormwood and many men die of the water because they are made bitter. Still man refuses to turn to God and ask for forgiveness.

The fourth angel sounds his trumpet and a third part of the sun is smitten, and a third part of the moon and the third part of the stars, so that a third part of them are darkened and the day doesn't shine not for a third part of it, and the night does likewise. Now at this point of time an angel is sent by the Lamb to fly through the heavens with a loud voice crying out a warning to all living men on earth because of what is about to happen when the remaining angels sound their trumpets. Man continues to refuse to turn from their sins and repent.

Now, by the command of the Lamb, the fifth angel sounds his trumpet and a star falls from heaven and a great key is given to him, which is the key to the bottomless pit.

This fallen star opens the door to the bottomless pit and a great smoke, like the smoke of a great furnace, rises from the pit and it darkens the sun and the air by the smoke coming out of the pit. However, this great darkness caused by the smoke is still not enough for man to turn to the Lamb and ask for forgiveness.

Out of the smoke come forth locusts upon the earth with the power of scorpions. They are commanded not to hurt the grass or any green thing, neither trees. This is very contrary to the nature of locusts, as we all know a swarm of locusts will destroy any green thing in their way. These are under strict orders not to harm the grass, tree, or any green thing but to attack and sting those who have the mark of the beast on his forehead. Even though they are very poisonous they are commanded not to kill but to cause these men to be tormented as a scorpion when it poisons a man.

In the days of their judgment men will seek to die but will not be able to, death will flee from them. The description of these locusts has caused men to wonder what they really are. They appear like horses ready for battle with crowns on their heads and faces as men. They have hair like women and teeth like lions. They have breastplates as breastplates of iron, and their wings sound like many chariots. Their tails are like scorpions with stings in their tails that can hurt men for five months.

Their king is the angel over the bottomless pit whose name is Abaddon in the Hebrew tongue and Apollyon in Greek. One woe has passed and there are two more woes that are to come. Once more the Lamb of God is giving man an opportunity to repent and come back to God, but man refuses to.

When the sixth angel sounds his trumpet a great voice is heard from the four horns of the altar which is before God. This voice speaks to the sixth angel who has the trumpet to loose the four angels bound in the great river of Euphrates. These angels, which are loosed, were prepared for an hour and a day and a month and a year to slay the third part of men.

Next we see the armies of horsemen which number two hundred thousand, thousand. These horsemen have breastplates of fire and smoke and brimstone and jacinth. The heads of the horses are as heads of lions and out of their mouths issue fire and smoke, and brimstone. These strange warriors destroy one third part of men by the fire, smoke, and brimstone that came out of their mouths, for their power was in their mouths and in their tails, for their tails have heads of serpents with which they hurt men.

The rest of the men, which are not killed by these plagues, still refuse to repent of the works of their hands so as not to worship devils and idols of gold and silver, and brass, and stone, and of wood. Neither would they repent of their murders, nor of their sorceries, nor of their fornications, nor of their thefts.

Finally, the great angel comes down from heaven clothed with a cloud and a rainbow is upon his head. He told the apostle John that in the days the voice of the seventh angel begins to sound, the mystery of God should be finished as he has declared to his servants and the prophets.

Next we see the Lamb of God standing on Mount Zion and with him the hundred and forty-four thousand having the Lamb's Father's name written on their forehead. We do not see the Lamb of God again. Instead the next time we see Him as He is in *Revelation 19:11*. It is not the Messiah of peace sitting on the horse; it is the conquering King of kings, the Lion of Judah.

We will address this side of the Messiah; however, I want to view the various portrayals of Christ found in the Scriptures. In many instances we can get stuck at one of the pictures of Jesus we are comfortable with and keep that image always before us.

CHAPTER SIX

••••••••••••••••••••••••

Favorite Images of Christ

The first we hear of the Messiah is in *Genesis 3:15* where God speaks to the serpent and tells him that he is cursed above all cattle and beasts of the earth. He also tells the serpent He will put enmity between him and the woman and between his seed and her seed. The seed of the woman would bruise the head of the serpent, and the seed of the serpent would bruise the heel of the seed of the woman.

Now we understand that the serpent is Satan who bruised the heel of Jesus at the crucifixion; in turn, Jesus bruised the head of Satan, meaning He took all of the power of Satan from him and this truly happened when Jesus descended into Paradise where the souls of the righteous were.

Even though they died righteous, they could not enter in heaven, the kingdom of God, because the price of redemption had not been paid as yet. When the Lamb shed

His blood on the cross, He paid the price so
when he rose from the dead he emptied
Paradise of all the righteous that was there
and that particular area was completely
empty. It's true! Satan's power as well as
death, hell and the grave was taken from
them forever.

There is also another meaning to
Genesis 3:15. The seed of the serpent was
not Satan because the serpent was Satan in
the shape of a serpent. The seed spoken of
was the antichrist that Christ will absolutely
destroy by the brightness of his coming. If
you doubt Satan was the serpent refer to
Revelation 20:2.

Another picture of the Messiah
people have is the seed of David, the greater
Son of David who would sit on the throne of
His Father and rule from Jerusalem forever
and would judge the nations of the world,
ruling over them and bringing peace to the
world. Now this is the Messiah my people,
the Jews have, it is the picture of the
conquering Messiah, the King who would
deliver Israel from all their enemies.

It is a beautiful picture of the Messiah, but the vision of the conquering Messiah, the Lion of the tribe of Judah blinds them to the first coming of the Messiah, the Lamb of God who takes away the sins of the world and redeems man back to His Father. *Psalm 89:26* speaks of the seed of David who would cry out to the Lord, "Thou are my Father and my God, and the rock of my salvation." God proclaims He would make His first born higher than the kings of the earth.

This is a great picture but because my people stop there with this vision of Christ, they could not see the suffering Messiah, only the conquering one. This caused them to miss the coming of the Messiah when He first came.

I want to know Christ--yes, to know the power of his resurrection and participation in his sufferings, becoming like him in his death.

Philippians 3:10

CHAPTER SEVEN

••••••••••••••••••••••••••••••

The Infant in the Manger

The next vision of the Messiah is that of the little infant born in a cave in the field of Bethlehem of Judea. It is also the field where the Passover lambs were born. During the spring season sheep give birth in the field and shepherds stand watch and also inspect the lambs born to see if they were worthy to be the Passover lamb.

On the night of Christ's birth, the only lamb born in that field was God's Passover Lamb who passed the inspection of the shepherds. They proclaimed Him without blemish. This sweet vision of the Messiah is as a sweet infant in the arms of His young virgin mother. It is the image of the Messiah that thousands of people have of the Lord Jesus.

This is the image many people are taught to pray and worship, especially Him and His mother. They made her equal to Him as a redeemer and intercessor. This picture of the Messiah and His mother keep millions of Catholics in bondage.

CHAPTER EIGHT

••••••••••••••••••••••••••••••

The Young Jesus

The next picture of the Messiah is found in *Luke 2:45-51*. It is of twelve-year-old Jesus who is discovered missing by His parents. After a three-day search they found Him in the temple in the midst of the doctors, both listening and asking questions that astonished everyone who heard Him.

Many hold on to this image of the Messiah. They talk about His wisdom how He confounded the doctors and how they could not answer Him.

Yes, this is a beautiful image of Jesus when He was a young man and even then His knowledge of His Father's words was amazing but we still need to let go of this picture and see Christ in His fullness.

For from his fullness we have all received, grace upon grace.
John 1:16

CHAPTER NINE

....

Jesus' Baptism

The next image of Jesus is at His baptism by His cousin John. We see Him baptized, and when He comes out of the water the Holy Spirit descends on Him as a dove and the voice of the Father proclaims Him as His beloved Son in whom He is well pleased. Then He is led into the wilderness to be tempted by the adversary in which Jesus overcomes by the word.

When Jesus went into the wilderness, He went in as Jesus, the Son of man. He endured forty days of testing, being obedient in all things, standing face to face with the adversary and defeating him. Jesus was at His weakest physically and emotionally. His enemy was at his strongest. When Jesus came out of the wilderness, every demon that encountered Him knew they were facing Yeshua Ben Elohim, Jesus the Son of the most high God. All of His enemies feared Him.

Since He victoriously completed His testing and trials without complaint and murmuring, all power in heaven and earth was His. Now the Lamb had more power than was needed to destroy His enemy, instead He chose to be merciful and have compassion on them.

It is amazing because at any time, if the Lamb wanted to, He could have asked His Father for twelve legions of angels and He would have sent them. (*Matthew 26:53*) To think that one angel by himself killed 185,000 men of war, what would 12,000 angels have been able to do? This was not the way of the Lamb; His way was the way of the Father to obey him in all things even death on the cross. (*2 Kings 19:35*)

What a beautiful picture of the Lamb! He is gentle, forgiving, and there are no acts of retaliation against those who despise Him. Now this is one picture of the Lamb of God we should be happy to follow. Christ has strength to overcome the enemy, but He has compassion to forgive and love those who came to Him.

CHAPTER TEN

••••••••••••••••••••••••••••

The Young Rabbi

Now see Him as a young rabbi beginning His teaching ministry. He is thirty years of age, which gives Him the right to speak openly and in the public and to voice His opinion on the daily topic. He is convinced He is right, for every word He speaks comes from the Father and they are not His own. (*John 14:24*)

He speaks with compassion, mercy, grace, and love. Even when His enemies came against Him they leave saying, "never has any man spoken like this one." This kind gentle young rabbi gathers the multitude to Him by His love and kindness. In (*Matthew 4:23-24*) Jesus went about all of Galilee teaching in their synagogues and preaching the gospel of the kingdom, healing all manners of diseases among the people and His fame went throughout all Syria. They brought unto Him all sick people that were taken with diver diseases and torments, those who were possessed with devils, those who were lunatic, and those who had the palsy. He healed them all.

In *Matthew 8* you see His great compassion as the man with leprosy comes to Him and asks to be healed. The Lord does not rebuke him or tell him to stay away because he was unclean. No, He simply said, 'I will', and touched him and the man is instantly made whole.

What happens next is simply amazing! Unlike today's preachers, Jesus told the man to go and tell no one who had healed him. Today's preachers would have had the man on every Christian television station there was giving his testimony about how he was healed by this preacher. This was not the way of the Lamb of God

He even had time for those not of His faith. (*Matthew 8:5-19*) This young rabbi had no material possessions of His own, yet everything He had He freely gave to those in need. In (*Luke 19:41*) we see His compassion as He weeps for Jerusalem. In (*John 11:35*) He weeps at the tomb of His friend Lazarus because of the people's unbelief. You see first hand the love He has for His people and for anyone who would come to Him. He would turn no one away.

All those the Father gives me will come to me, and whoever comes to me I will never drive away. John 6:37

CHAPTER ELEVEN

•••••••••••••••••••••••••••••••••

The Lamb on the Donkey

We see people on both sides of the road waving palm branches and shouting, "Hosanna: Blessed is the king of Israel that comes in the name of the Lord." We see the average citizens of Jerusalem celebrating the Lamb's entrance into the city on the colt of an ass. The religious society reacts in hostility and jealously over the Lamb who came to redeem them from their sins. The teachers of the law, the Pentateuch, the Haftarah, the prophets, and the ones who were responsible to teach the people about the Messiah were quite angry.

He was their King and Savior yet they were blind to who this young rabbi was. The one they waited so long for was now in their very midst, and instead of celebrating the greater Son of David who would sit on His Father's throne forever, they were planning His death.

We can see the lonely road the Lamb had chosen to walk for our sake. Once more the Father's voice is heard giving glory to the Son. Can you feel His sadness as He stands with His head lowered, knowing that the judgment of the world has come to pass? The prince of this world will be cast out. Kingdoms have come into conflict and the adversary will lose his authority and keys will be given over. The Lamb will die, beaten and bruised and alone; however, in His death He will bring life to millions throughout the ages. (*John 12:28:33*)

The Lamb is calling out to those who would believe in Him to come to Him. He warns them that the words He is speaking are not His words but the words the Father has said unto Him. (*John 12:44-59*)

We see the Lamb kneeling at the feet of His disciples to wash their feet. By doing this He is showing all of us who are called to preach the kingdom message that we must first serve God then others. We are called to serve and give, not to dictate and take from the sheep. What an awesome picture of the Lamb! He who created all things by His words, and He who came to take away the sins of mankind was kneeling in front of a handful of ordinary men and washing their feet. (*John 1:1-3*)

This is one of my favorite pictures of Him, and I pray for the grace to be able to copy it in my own ministry. It shows to me the love and compassion the Lamb had for mankind, and to the extent He would be willing to go to give man a chance to come to Him.

It is a short period of time before Judas Iscariot would betray Him for thirty pieces of silver. And knowing that Judas Iscariot would betray Him, He still kneels in front of him, taking the role of a servant, and bathing his feet. What a wonderful Savior! Only a Lamb could be so graceful and so willing to forgive. The Lion would not have been so kind. It is not in his nature.

Can you imagine a lion sitting passively as you pull his mane and strike him in the face as in the case of Aslan the lion in the Chronicles of Narnia by C.S. Lewis? Aslan, the lion, acted like a lamb until his resurrection where he let his lion nature come forth. The Lamb of God will do the same in His return to earth as the Lion of the tribe of Judah.

The Lamb is sitting at the last Passover supper surrounded by the disciples. They are ready to eat when Jesus explains that He will be betrayed by one of His own. They are all shocked and begin asking, "Lord is it I?"

Jesus said, "The one who dips his hand in the dish with Me, he is the one." Even though Jesus knows Judas Iscariot will betray Him, He still loves Him. It's the nature of the Lamb to love at all times and to be gentle to everyone. As natural men we cannot understand this gentle nature. Even after many of us are born again we don't fully understand this nature.

I have met a few people who have reach this point of maturity. The first person was the wonderful African American sister, Beatrice, and her wonderful giant of a husband, James, who prayed for twenty-six years that God would have mercy on me and save me. The second was my grandfather on my father's side who loved me when no one else did. Thirdly was Pastor Babosa who taught me the power in Jesus' name.

The fourth was Dr. Leonard Heroo of Zion Bible Institute who spoke hope into my life and encouragement when everyone else was finding fault. Finally there was Apostle Robert Ewing from Waco, Texas. No gentler man could be found. He was so humble, and so much of the power of the Holy Spirit could be seen in this little man.

I have come to understand that in meekness there is great strength. It is sad because people misunderstand meekness as weakness.

The Lamb of God is meek
and humble, but NEVER weak.

CHAPTER TWELVE

•••••••••••••••••••••••••••••••••

The Beaten Lamb

After the last supper Jesus goes to the Garden of Gethsemane to pray for He knew His time was up and soon He would be taken, beaten and then crucified. Jesus needed to be alone with His Father to pray for He knew what was about to happen. He asked for this cup to be removed if it could be.

Three times He was told it couldn't. (*Luke 22:42; Mark 14:36; Matthew 26:39*) It was the destiny of the Lamb to die for the sins of the world. No other man would be able to do it, for only Jesus was born without sin and only He could restore man back to His Father. Only His pure blood could pay the price of sin and only the stripes on His back could heal all of our sickness.

Jesus is delivered to Pilate because the Jews couldn't put any man to death. These people felt they had power over Him. He let them know this when He told the high priest that all He had to do was ask the Father and He would send twelve legions of angels to help Him. With all this help at His hand, He made the choice not to resist but to endure the pain and torture. The high priest struck Him. The priest and the people spit on Him and plucked His beard. The soldier beat His back, ripping it open, and they drove a crown of thorns into His head.

They let a murderer go free in His place, and now with two others He was taken to the place of the skull where He would be crucified between the two thieves. There, as the crowd gathered to see these three men crucified, they see the man in the middle is so different from the other two. One of the thieves mocks Him and the other tells him to stop for the one in the middle is guiltless.

He calls to Jesus, "Lord, please forgive and let me come be with you." This man, a thief, becomes the first to be saved because of the cross. God's plan of salvation is bearing fruit even before the death and resurrection of Jesus. Even on the cross the Lamb was looking for those who need His help. He looks down and sees His own mother standing in the crowd. He sees John the beloved and gives to him the care of His mother.

He is now ready to lay down His life as an offering. As He dies a miracle happens to open their eyes to who He was. The moment He dies the curtain in the temple is torn in half from the top to the bottom and the earthquake and the rocks are rent. The graves of the righteous are opened and many bodies of the saints arise and come out of their graves to show themselves to many.

It's unbelievable but many closed their hearts to the miracle of God. In this image of the Lamb, He is hanging on a cross, filled with love and mercy. We see His love for others, He forgave the thief, the temple curtain is torn from the top to bottom, the graves of the righteous are opened and they go into the city.

Finally the Lamb sends His spirit home to His Father. He descends to hell to the side of Paradise where the righteous ones are gathered together.

Adam, Abraham, Solomon, David, Isaac, Jacob, Moses and Joshua and many, many more know now after a very short time they will be taken into the presence of God. They will never be in that place ever again for now hell will expand and this place will not be needed any more.

So now from the moment of the Lord's resurrection, the righteous man goes straight to be with the Lord after he dies and the unrighteous man goes to hell.

What horror will the proud and arrogant self-righteous people in that day feel in the end times? They refused to believe He was the Messiah who died to set the people free. Now they will be face to face with the Son of God, the Lamb who came to take away the sins of many. They will know all hope for them is gone. The grave would be their home until the Day of Judgment. Then they, along with everyone who didn't believe that Jesus was Lord, including Satan, the antichrist and the false prophet will spend eternity in the lake of fire.

Can you picture the adversary's face when he sees the Lamb standing there in Paradise and heading to the gates of hell to take from him, death, hell, and the grave their keys, their power, and their authority? Imagine their conversation: Satan is speaking to Death and says, "Hello, I got Jesus beaten, betrayed, and crucified. All you had to do, Death, was take His life and hold Him so Grave could hold Him down. What went wrong? Death! All you had to do was take Him when He died and turn Him over to Grave who would put Him with all the others where we could mock and torment Him anytime we wanted!"

"It wasn't my fault," replies Death. "It's not my fault He didn't have a spirit when I got to Him. Actually I was confused. I thought he might be an Anakim or Nephilim. Anyway, I did give Him over to the grave where He would be kept just like everyone else. How was I to know He could send His spirit home to His Father?"

"You're such an idiot, Death! This is the Son of God we're talking about. All we had to do was follow the plan. He would be beaten then killed. How could He come out with victory in all things?"

"Grave! Do you still have the rest of Him still in you?"

"Yes Satan, I still have the body. It is not going anywhere. Watch and see how good I am. What about you Hades? As soon as He was taken in, I had our imp search all entrances. There is no way He is getting out to fulfill the fable of the resurrected Lord." Grave laughs. He is delighted at their carefully laid plan.

Suddenly Grave begins to sweat and shake uncontrollably. He cannot believe what he is seeing. "Wait a minute! Did I just see a light in the vast darkness of hell? There has never been light here in hell. Hades! Where is this light coming from? Death! Do you know? Grave? Somebody answer me!"

It is coming from the Lamb, slain for the redemption of all men who they are trying to enslave through sin. It is coming from the very Son of God. This is the One, oh adversary, who will crush your head and take away your power and the keys of death, hell, and the grave. Can you imagine what these four enemies of God and man must have felt when the Lamb walked up to them and took the keys from their hands?

Can you imagine the terror in Satan's mind when a Lamb defeated him?

He has yet to face the Lion of Judah

CHAPTER THIRTEEN

••••••••••••••••••••

The Resurrected Lamb

We have a new picture of the Lamb. It has only been seventy-two hours since He was beaten, crucified, died and buried in a borrowed tomb. Then He descended into Abraham's bosom surrounded by the Old Testament saints and the thief who had been crucified and died alongside Him.

While there He preached to them, who were sometime disobedient and then He took away the keys (authority) of death, hell, and the grave. (*1 Peter 3:18-20*) We can proclaim in confidence, "O death where is thy sting? O grave where is your victory?" (*1 Corinthians 15:55*)

After defeating His enemies on their stronghold. He rose from the grave leading in His train those who were once in captivity, because the price of sin hadn't yet been paid for. After bringing His treasures home and laying them at His Father's feet, He returns to show Himself to Mary Magdalene in *John 20:16*.

Later, on the first day of the week, He shows Himself to all of His disciples except for Thomas. After eight days all the disciples, including Thomas, were together and Jesus appears unto them. Jesus shows Himself again to the disciples at the Sea of Tiberias. (*John 21:1*) Two disciples see Him on the Road to Emmaus. (*Luke 24:13*)

Finally, in the presence of the disciples and others, He ascends on high to sit at the right hand of the Father Most High. From there He shall become the judge of the living and the dead. For now He is interceding on our behalf. He is preparing a place for us in His Father's kingdom.

CHAPTER FOURTEEN

••

Behold the Lion of the Tribe of Judah

Revelation 5:5 introduces us to the other nature of the Lord Jesus, the mighty Lion of the tribe of Judah. The elder speaking to John tells him not to weep for the Lion of the tribe of Judah, the root of David, hath prevailed to open the book and to loose the seals thereof.

Israel prophesies concerning his sons. He said of Judah, "Thou art he whom the brethren shall praise: thy hand shall be on the necks of thine enemies: thy Father's children shall bow down before thee. Judah is a lion whelp: from the prey, my son, thou art gone up: he stooped down; he crouched as a lion, and as an old lion that shall rouse him up. The scepter shall not depart from Judah, nor a lawgiver from between his feet until Shiloh comes and unto him shall the gathering of the people be. (*Genesis 49:8-10*)

There is not much written about the Lion of Judah as there is about the Lamb of God who would take away the sins of the world. We know it was very necessary that the Lamb should come to make a way of salvation. The Lamb had to come to be a sacrifice so that whosoever believed in Him would not perish but would have life eternal.

It was the responsibility of the Lamb to provide forgiveness, redemption, and restoration. He would hold back the hand of God's judgment on a rebellious world. If the Lamb did not come before the Lion, there would have been no need for the Lamb to come at all because everything would have been destroyed.

We have followed the wonderful life of the Lamb. For over thirty years the earth was blessed with the presence of the Lamb walking the streets of Israel from Bethlehem to Jerusalem. We watched as He opened the eyes of the blind, the ears of the deaf and loosed the tongues of the speechless. We watched in amazement as He raised the dead, healed the sick, cleansed the leper and cast out devils.

We stood in awe at the wisdom of His words; surely one wiser than Solomon was among us. He was kind to the outcast and poor. He fed the hungry and gave understanding of God's word and the ways of the kingdom. Like so many good things in life, we are always too busy to enjoy them when we have them. When they are gone, we wish we had spent more time with them, to enjoy them when we had the chance.

It is the same with the Lamb. Now that He has returned to His Father and to His throne, we wish we could have at least one day to spend with Him and to listen to His wisdom. Those days of Him physically being here on earth with us are gone; however, we have His words in which we can find truth, wisdom, knowledge, and eternal life. Don't do with His words what our ancestors did with Him by ignoring Him and substituting religion for relationship.

Religion will keep us from knowing Him and His word. It leads us to damnation. Relationship on the other hand will give us a hunger for Him and His words and lead us to salvation.

The Lamb has come and gone. His time is over. It is now time for the Lion of Judah, whose eyes are flames of fire (indication of purity), whose hair is white as snow (showing holiness) and whose feet are as brass (indicating He stands in judgment). This is a picture of Jesus standing in strength as a judge.

I believe we now begin to see the Lion emerge

....

Look at some of the characteristics of lions:

they are strong (Psalm 30:30); their teeth are powerful (*Job 4:10*); their paws are powerful (*1 Samuel 17:37*); they're fearless (*Proverbs 29:1*); stealthier (*Psalm 17:12*); frightening (*Ezra 19:7*); destructive (*1 Samuel 17:34, Micah 5:8*); and territorially protective (*Isaiah 31:4*). With all of its power, the lion is ultimately dependent on God (*Job 38:39-40, Psalm 104:21*) and he is answerable to God (*Job 4:10*).

God is described with a number of lion-like features

••

He is strong (*Isaiah 38:13*); fearless in protecting His own (*Isaiah 31:4*); stealthy in coming on His prey (*Jeremiah 49:19, Hosea 13:7*); frightening (*Hosea 11:10, Amos 3:38*); destructive (*Jeremiah 25:38, Lamentations 3:10, Hosea 5:14, 13:8*). The lion even appears as a title of God.

The image of the Lamb shows Christ as a willing sacrifice who came to restore man back to His Father. The image of the Lion shows Christ as the awesome conquering King that no enemy can stand against. Jesus is worthy to open the scroll because as the Lamb He conquered death, hell, and the grave. When He returns as the Lion of Judah, He will conquer and destroy all of His enemies.

When Jesus returns from heaven He will return in strength and power. No one will be able to stand against Him or prevail against Him. He, like the lion described in *Isaiah 38:13*, is more than able to break the bones of His enemies and will not be turned from them. The Lion of Judah will come down to protect His people and no one will be able to stop Him or turn Him away.

He, like the lion, will suddenly appear and when you expect Him the least. The Lord will hunt all of His enemies as a fierce lion. (*Job 10:16, Isaiah 42:13*) Scripture says, the Lord shall cry, yea, He shall roar.

It is said that the roar of a full grown African lion can be heard as far away as up to one mile and will produce so much fear in the heart of lesser animals as to completely paralyze them where they stand. If the image of the African lion can do that, what will happen when the mighty Lion of Judah roars with all His might?

Every one of his enemies will freeze with hopelessness and fear. All those who have been trying to imitate Him will know that their time is up and they will be revealed for the fake that they are. As it says in *Hosea 11:10*, "When the Lord roars it will be absolutely frightening every nerve in the human body will be affected by it, every bone in the body will shake uncontrollably. Every heart will be filled with feared."

Just like the roar of the lion, *the roar of the Lord will paralyze every being on the earth, above the earth and under the earth,* even in the sea. Every living creature will come to a complete stand still. There will be no atheist that day. The arrogance of the witches and cult members will come to an end. There will be no more excuses or lies. All the inner secrets of every heart will be exposed. The day that the Lord returns will be a day of darkness and great judgment.

The day of the Lord according to *Isaiah 2:12, 13* states "for the day of the Lord of hosts shall be upon every one that is proud and lofty and upon every one that is lifted up." *Isaiah 2:10-11* states "enter into the rock and hide thee into the dust for fear of the Lord and for the glory of His majesty. The lofty look of man shall be humbled and haughtiness of men shall bow down and the Lord alone shall be exalted in that day." Over and over again in *Isaiah 2* we are told that the arrogant man shall be humbled and the Lord alone will be lifted up. That man will try to hide from the Lord and His glory.

The next couple of scriptures will show us what it will be like when the Lord of lords and the King of kings leads His armies, which were in heaven with Him, to the earth and He returns as the Lion of Judah, the greater Son of David. The prophet Joel speaks of the day of the Lord. "Sanctify ye a fast call, a solemn assembly, gather the elders and all the inhabitants of the land unto the house of the Lord your God and cry unto the Lord. Alas for the day of the Lord is at hand, and as destruction from the Almighty shall it come. Is not the meat cut off before our eyes, yea, joy and gladness from the house of our God?" (*Joel 1:14-16*)

Joel 1:1, 2 states "blow ye the trumpet (shofar) in Zion and sound an alarm in My holy mountains, let all the inhabitants of the land tremble for the day of the Lord cometh for it is nigh at hand, a day of darkness and gloominess, a day of clouds and thick darkness." I know many people are praying for the day of the Lord to come.

I believe our prayer should be: Lord please rapture us before You come. I don't know about you but I prefer to be behind the Lion of Judah instead of in front of Him.

In *Joel 2:11* the prophet writes "and the Lord shall utter His voice before His armies for His camp is very great for He is strong that executeth His word for the day of the Lord is great and very terrible and who can abide it." The prophet Joel goes on to say the sun shall be turned into darkness and the moon into blood, before the great and terrible day of the Lord will come.

"Behold the day of the Lord cometh and the spoil shall be divided in the midst of thee for I will gather all nations against Jerusalem to battle; and the city shall be taken and the houses rifled and the woman ravished and half the city shall go forth into captivity and the residue shall be cut off from the city. And then shall the Lord go forth and fight against those nations as when He fought in the day of battle. (*Zechariah 14:1-3*)

The day of the Lord will definitely be a great and terrible day for those who have been left behind. In Revelation it states that blood will flow up to the bridle of a horse for two hundred furloughs. (*Revelation 14:20*) Isn't this amazing? There would be enough area to cover all of Jerusalem with the blood of men killed in battle on that terrible day of the Lord.

Joel 2 tells us that the Lord is merciful and kind and that after He chastises the people He will pour out His Spirit on all people and will show wonders in the heavens and in the earth, blood, and fire, and pillars of smoke. The sun will be turned into darkness and the moon into blood before the great and terrible day of the Lord comes. It shall come to pass that whosoever calls on the name of the Lord shall be saved. For Mount Zion, Jerusalem and His remnant shall be delivered as the Lord has said.

Once again the sun and moon shall be darkened and the stars shall withdraw their shining. The Lord shall also roar out of Zion and utter His voice from Jerusalem, and the heavens and the earth shall shake but

the Lord will be the hope of His people and
the strength of the children of Israel.

In *Zephaniah* the Lord continues to
give insight into what the day of the Lord
will be like. "The great day of the Lord is
near, it is near, and hasteth greatly, even
voice of the day of the Lord: the mighty men
shall cry there bitterly. That day is a day of
wrath, a day of trouble and distress, a day of
wasteness and desolation, a day of darkness
and gloominess, a day of clouds and thick
darkness. A day of the trumpet and alarm
against the fenced cities, and the high
towers. And I will bring distress upon men,
that they shall walk like blind men, because
they have sinned against the Lord: and their
blood shall be poured out as dust and their
flesh as the dung. Neither their silver nor
their gold shall be able to deliver them in the
day of the Lord's wrath; but the whole land
shall be devoured by the fire of His jealousy:
for He shall make even a speedy riddance of
all them that dwell in the land."
(*Zephaniah 1:14-18*)

In *Malachi 4* the Lord warns that the
day will come that shall burn as an oven and

all the proud yea and all that do wickedly shall be stubble and the day that comes will burn them up, saith the Lord of hosts, that it shall leave them neither roots or branches. In *Malachi 4:5, 6* the Lord says I will send Elijah the prophet before the coming of the great and terrible day of the Lord. And he shall turn the hearts of the fathers to the children and the hearts of the children to the fathers lest I come and smite the earth with a curse.

In *Matthew 11:10* the Lord calls John the Baptist, the messenger that was sent before Jesus to prepare the way for Him. Later on in *Matthew 11:14* Jesus goes as far as to call him Elias who was to come. However, I do not feel that this was the total fulfillment of *Malachi 4:5*. I believe that Elijah the prophet who never died shall some day in the future return with Enos (Enoch) to prepare the way of the Lord and to turn the hearts of the fathers to the children and the children to the father. More importantly to turn the hearts of both the fathers and the children to the Lord God and the good Lord will spare many from destruction

In the book of *Acts 2:14-21* Peter is standing and explaining to the crowd of people what they are seeing and hearing. Peter stated that this was the fulfillment of the promise made by God in the book of Joel where God promised to pour out His Spirit upon all flesh and that their sons and daughters would prophesy and their young men will see visions and their old men would dream dreams. And on My servant and on My handmaidens, I will pour out in these days My Spirit, and they will prophesy and I will show wonders in heaven above and signs in the earth beneath, blood and fire and vapor of smoke. The sun shall be turned into darkness and the moon into blood before the great and terrible day of the Lord. And it shall come to pass that whosoever calls on the name of the Lord shall be saved

It is so amazing to see the difference between the first advent and the second advent. In the first advent of the Lord when he came as the Lamb of God we see the infant in the manger surrounded by His mother and Joseph. We also see the heavenly host singing praises to the Highest and we see the shepherds coming to see this wonderful sight. The angels proclaim a Savior is born and peace to mankind. We see the heavens alive with joy and celebration. We see a star leading the Magi for two years to the very home where the two year old Jesus was.

As the *prophet Isaiah states in chapter 9:6-7* "For unto a child is born, unto us a Son is given and the government shall be upon His shoulders. His name shall be called Wonderful, Counselor, The Mighty God, The Everlasting Father, and The Prince of Peace. Of the increase of His government and peace there shall be no end."

It is absolutely amazing the difference between the Lamb and the Lion. In the case of the Lamb compassion and mercy was available to all who sought after it. Healing was provided, the needs of the children were met, and no one was sent away without their needs being met.

As the Lord said God will supply all of our needs according to His riches in glory in Christ Jesus. When the Lamb was walking the earth all could freely come to

Him. He would lift all of their burdens. He brought peace to all the troubled minds that were brought to Him.

How wonderful do you think it would have been when the Lamb was here if everyone, Jew or Gentile would have surrendered to him? What if we elected the King of kings and gave Him complete control of the earth? What if everybody took the advice of *Psalm 2* to kiss the Son before He became angry with him or her? When we look at what the scriptures show us about the Lord's patience and love for His creation it should cause us to love Him all the more.

It is unbelievable to think that God would be completely aware of all of the betrayal by His creation starting with Lucifer and then with Adam and Eve and finally with each of us. Yet He still made us and gave to us free will, the choice to obey or disobey.

Just as in the case of Israel, how many times did they turn their backs on God and go after idols? The blessings could have been Israel's if they had only kept their promises to God. It is so sad that Israel, who was meant to be a blessing to all nations because of their relationship with God and who called them to be a nation, substituted their relationship with God by living a religious life, which only leads to death and eternal separation. I can only pray that we who call ourselves Christians can learn from their mistakes. Please always remember, Israel's religion blinded them to the coming of the Lamb.

Here He was among them as it was promised and because of their blindness they missed it. Three heathen kings knew more about the signs of His coming than the religious leaders of the time.

We are extremely fortunate where it states in *Ephesians 2:4*, "God is rich in mercy, for His great love wherewith He loved us. Even when we were dead in sins, hath quickened us together with Christ, (by grace ye are saved); and hath raised us up together and made us sit together in heavenly places in Christ Jesus."

The mercies of the Lamb of God are beyond the ability of the unregenerate mind of sinful man to understand. How could God love us so much that He chose us in Him before the foundation of the world, that we should be holy and without blame before Him in love? All through the Old Testament we see the grace and mercies of God being shown to a rebellious people. In the New Testament we see an increase of God's mercies and grace as it is extended to both the Jew and the Gentile.

We see the love of the Lamb everywhere in the Old and the New Testament; moreover, we see the bloody hoof prints of the Lamb from Genesis to Jude. It is in Revelation, however that we see the beginning of the transformation from Lamb to Lion. In Revelation 5 the Lion of the tribe of Judah is found worthy to open the book and loose the seven seals.

Then we see the Lamb, not the Lion, taking the book out of the right hand of Him who is sitting on the throne.

We see all of heaven beginning to celebrate and to give glory and honor unto the Lamb. This includes the holy angels, every beast, and all the elders are joined by every creature, which is in heaven, and on the earth, and under the earth, and such as, are in the seas and all that are in them. They all begin to give praise and honor and glory and power unto Him who sits on the throne and unto the Lamb forever and ever.

It is the Lamb who begins to open the seven seals. From Revelation 6 through *Revelation 19* we see the wrath of the Lamb being poured out upon the enemies of God. It changes in Revelation 19:11 where we see another white horse with a person sitting on it who is called faithful and true and in righteousness He doth judge and make war.

His eyes are once again like flames of fire, and on His head are many crowns and He has a name written that no man knows, but He Himself. He is clothed with vesture dipped in blood: and His name is called the Word of God.

The armies of heaven follow Him on white horses clothed in fine linen, white and clean and out of the mouth of Him who sits on the white horse goes forth a sharp sword that He uses to smite the nations and He shall rule them with a rod of iron: He treadeth the wine press of the fierceness and the wrath of Almighty God. On this rider's vesture and on His thigh, a name is written King of kings and Lord of lords.

This is the Lion, the conquering Messiah, the one who comes to establish His kingdom forever. He comes in great strength and power to overthrow all of His enemies. Not only does He defeat all His enemies who gather together to try to defeat Him, but also He takes the antichrist and the false prophet and casts them alive into the lake of fire. Satan is taken by a strong angel and is cast into the bottomless pit for a thousand years.

It is amazing that as we look at *Revelation* it is hard to see where the Lamb of God ends and the Lion of Judah begins. I firmly believe this is true because the Lamb of God, who takes away the sins of the world and restores man back to God, is the very same being known as the Lion of the tribe of Judah who comes forward to destroy the enemies of God and His people.

I know there are many different pictures of the second coming of Jesus and many teachings about the rapture. As far as I am concerned what is important is that we believe Jesus is returning as He has promised He would. It is my prayer that we are ready for Him and for His kingdom to be established forever and that we are with Him forever.

I pray that religion does not blind the eyes of man once again so that he is caught by surprise when the Lamb of God returns to the earth He created as the Lion of the tribe of Judah. Our eternal destiny and the destiny of our loved ones all depends on the decision we make today.

What will you do with this man called Jesus? Will you accept the offer of salvation given to you by the Lamb of God who took away the sins of the world or will you reject the free gift of salvation and restoration? Will you end up with eternal separation and damnation when the Lion of Judah comes as the judge of the earth and all that is on it?

Heaven and hell are real. I have been in both places. I was in heaven for two hours and in hell for what seemed like eternity. In both instances God allowed them to happen. I cannot wait to go back to heaven when my work is done here but I promise you I never want to return to hell even for a short period of time.

I've heard so many people joking that since all of their friends will be in hell, it will just be one big party. Let me tell you from experience, there are no parties going on in hell. All you will hear is weeping, moaning and crying. All you will see is complete darkness. You cannot even see your hand in front of your face. You will feel complete loneliness and absolute dread and terror because you know that hell is only a holding place for the unrighteous until the Day of Judgment.

Then will come the horror of standing before the Judge of the whole world knowing that very shortly when you are face to face with Him, because of your refusal to believe Him and accept Him into your life, you will get what you thought you always wanted, eternal separation from Him. You will watch death, hell, and the grave, along with the fake prophet and the antichrist being thrown into the lake of fire alive.

As you're watching them you'll know that your turn will be coming up. Now you may say, "I do not believe in this." Well I can say, "I don't believe in gravity." That is until I fall off a tall building. It doesn't matter what I believe or don't believe about gravity I still will fall down.

It is the same concept about God and His word. You may say you don't believe in God or in His word. You may even teach others that there is no God and that man is the top of the evolutionary chain, but one second after you die you will be absolutely sure that there is a God and His word is real.

You will know that the eternal separation that is about to take place is your fault alone for you will see that God has done all He could to keep you from having to be condemned and cast away. In World War II there was a saying in the armed forces that stated, "There are no atheists in a fox hole." Because of my time in hell I can firmly declare, "There is no atheist in hell." You may joyfully proclaim as the communist did that you do not need God or religion to get by. It is your right to believe what you want. God did make you with a free will. The truth is whether you choose to believe or not to believe.

What we do with this gift of free will in the spiritual reflect what we do with it in the physical. If I come to a red light I have the free will to ignore it and go through it endangering others as well as myself.

If I cause an accident and someone is hurt I will be arrested and brought in front of a judge who will determine my punishment. Sure we can tell the judge we have a free will; therefore, we can do what we want and make our own decisions. The judge will simply acknowledge your free will, and then he will tell you that you abused the gift and caused someone else to be hurt.

The judge will look at you and say, "I also have free will. I can let you go or I can sentence you to prison. Therefore, I am activating my free will and sending you to prison because you chose to use your free will to break the law by running a red light and causing an accident which resulted in two other people being hospitalized." It will be the same with God on the Day of Judgment.

He will simply acknowledge that you have a free will. You made your own choice to disobey Him and not believe in Him and His Son, who as a Lamb chose to surrender His free will in order to restore fallen man back to me.

With your free will you choose to be separate from Me? Now you are getting your very own heart's desire. You will be separated from Me and have Me completely out of your life. You are forcing Me to do what I do not want but I have to keep My word. I sentence you to eternal separation from Me, My Son and all these Christians that drove you crazy.

Instead of meeting the Lamb who came to save you from sin, the world, the flesh and the devil, **you must meet the Lion** who came to defeat all of the enemies of My Father and His people. You could have been one of the people who will be with Him forever. Now He has to condemn you and send you to the lake of fire where you will see Him no more.

Please people, while there is still time to make a choice using our free will; choose to accept the Lamb of God's offer of eternal life and companionship with Him. Do not be one who will be facing the Lion who is to come to judge the world and destroy the enemies of His Father.

. It is absolutely true God loved the world that He sent His only begotten Son that whosoever would believe need not perish but have eternal life forever more.

CHAPTER FIFTEEN

••••••••••••••••••••••

God is a God of Love

True love corrects as well as hugs. If you have a son or daughter and they were always disobeying you no matter how much you show them love and mercy, there has to come a day of correction. No matter how much they say they have rights, as you are correcting them you can inform them the only true right they have in your home is to obey your rules and instructions while they live in your home.

God is no different than you when it comes to this. I know He loves us so much He wants to bless us and not to have to chastise us all the time. It was never God's intention to have man placed in hell or the lake of fire. These were created for the devil and his followers. God has done all He could to save us. Now it is your choice to choose the gift of salvation or the curse of separation and damnation. God is waiting to see whom you choose – the Lamb of life or the Lion of judgment.

Brothers and sisters it is not my intention to scare anyone. I remember as a child how bad I felt when people would try to scare me into doing what they wanted me to do. I am just trying to show you the difference between the Lamb of God who died on the cross for us willingly and the Lion of the tribe of Judah who is coming to destroy the enemies of our God. The Lamb came and walked among His people for thirty-three years doing good and blessing people, healing them, and giving life to all who would take it.

We are glad that He came to save us from death, hell, and the grave and to bring us home to be with the Father to enjoy time in heaven and then rule and reign with Him on the new earth. This is the nature of the Lamb, but it is not the same with the Lion. He will come to destroy the kingdom of Satan, the antichrist and the false prophet. Anyone not standing with the Lamb will be dying with the Lion. The choice is up to you. I pray with everything within me you make the right choice.

It is a good thing to stay loyal to your church, especially if the pastor is a faithful shepherd who loves his sheep, and teaches and preaches the word. But if you are in a church that teaches religion instead of relationship I would strongly urge you to find a church no matter how small it may be that can teach on relationship and introduce you to Christ personally.

We need more than to know about Him, we need to know Him

....

We need to hear His commands and His directions as Moses did.(*Numbers 9:8*) With the help of the Lamb who comes to live in us we will have the strength to stand against the enemy of our soul. Remember the words of Paul the Apostle when he said, "It is no longer I that lives but Christ that lives this life through me."

Paul, in speaking to *the Galatians in 2:20*, said, "I am crucified with Christ, nevertheless I live yet not I but Christ liveth in me and the life in which I now live in the flesh I live by the faith of the Son of God

who loved me and gave Himself for me."
Then in *Colossians 1:27* Paul wrote, "to
whom God would make known what is the
riches of the glory of this mystery among the
Gentiles; which is Christ in you the hope of
glory."

We don't walk alone. The Lord is
always with us. He has promised to never
leave us and to abide in us forever. He
promised while He was here on earth to send
His Holy Spirit to lead us and guide us in all
the things of heaven and of God. He gave
our battle gear to wear and the weapons of
warfare so that we can stand strong in the
battle and not fall.

He gave us the weapons

He gave us the weapons we desperately
need. *(2 Corinthians 10:4)* He gave the
word to use it, which is our sword. *(John
17:14-17)* He gave us prayer *Matthew 6:9-
13* so we can pray for one another. He gave
us praise *(Psalms 22:3)* to give Him thanks
for all He has done for us. Finally He gave
us worship *(Psalms 95:6)* so we can

fellowship with Him and Him with us. God promises to always dwell in our praise.

He said, "I inhabit the praises of My people. *(Psalm 22:3) "* It is amazing to get to know God. It took the strength of the Lion to let men beat Him and nail Him on the cross, but it took the compassion of the Lamb to hold Him there and then ask the Father to forgive His enemies for they did not know what they were doing. It took the love of the Lamb to give us the bread and water of life.

It took unbelievable mercy to provide a way back to God while we weren't believers. When we were far off, He loved us and made a way for us to come home. Like our Lord and Savior, Jesus, we too have a double nature. Since we are now under the second Adam we have His nature and attributes.

We are both the lion and lamb

....

The problem is we don't know when to be the lion and when to be the lamb. As you are talking to men you must always be the lamb, which is being kind, loving, merciful, and always willing to be a blessing.

However, with the enemy, in your prayer closet, you let the roar of the Lion be heard. Give no quarters to the enemy. Do not let him snatch one soul from you.

Do not allow him to take one more addict, one drunk or any soul you are praying for. Have faith in God. He hears our cry . *Psalm 34:17*

Submit yourselves to God. The devil will flee from you. *James 4:7*

Tell him, "the Lord rebukes you and I agree with that rebuke in Jesus' name." Pray for your enemies so they will become your friends. *Matthew 5:44*

Your prayers can make heaven overcrowded. Your lack of prayer can make heaven empty of souls. You were meant to win for the Lord. Only you can do what God has created you for, not me, not your friends, not your parents, only YOU!

God bless, and keep a watch out for the Lion. Hopefully you will be coming back with Him and not facing Him in judgment.

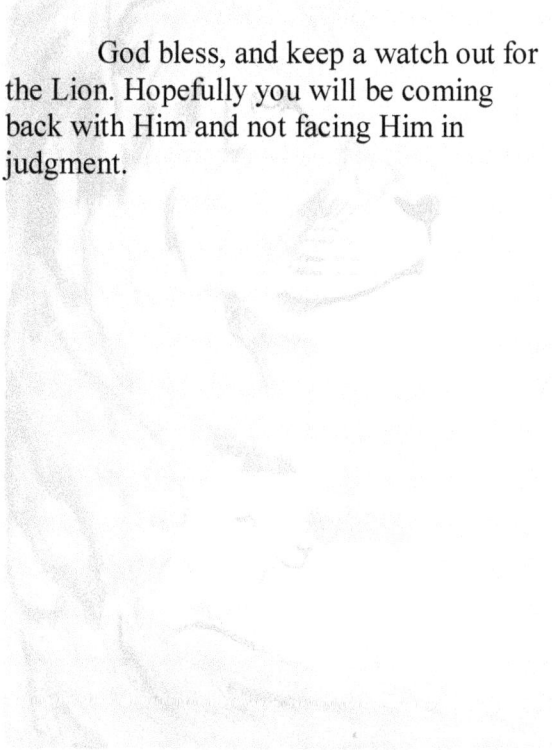

2 Timothy 2:24-25
And the Lord's servant must not quarrel; instead he must be kind to everyone, able to teach, not resentful.

Those who oppose him he must gently instruct, in the hope that God will grant him repentance leading them to a knowledge of the truth

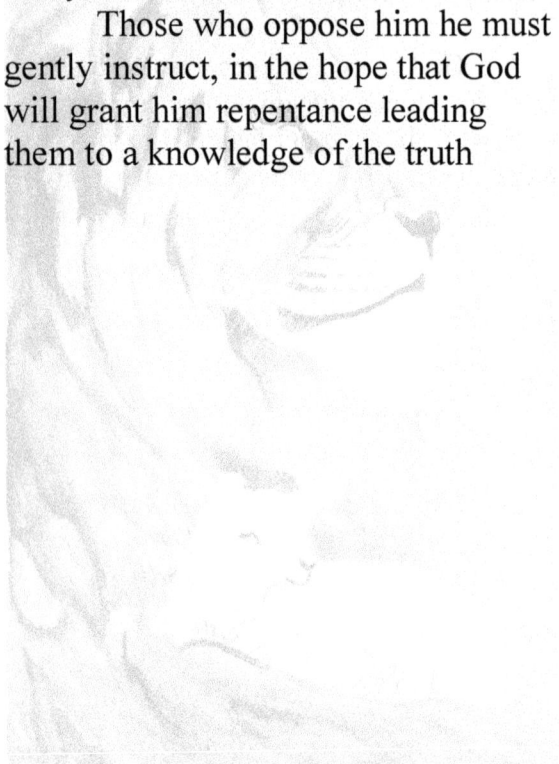

ABOUT THE AUTHOR

Dr. Henry Lewis is the President of an Apostolic
International ministry called Joshua International.
Joshua International offers Biblical Leadership
Training and Spiritual Over comers material. Henry
Lewis is a Sicilian Jew and a descendent of Andrew
Murray.

He is married to his wife, Patricia, for over 42 years.
They have been in ministry since 1980 and have two
children.

Dr. Lewis has authored 10 books. The first book
called A Quest for Spiritual Power is now translated
in Arabic and in French.
The Arabic book was printed in Egypt and the French
book was assembled and translated in Switzerland
and printed in France.

Dr. Lewis is a sought-after speaker and author,
teaching at churches and conferences along with
numerous TV guest media outlets teaching on
subjects such as: spiritual warfare, revival,
transformation, revelation, transformational prayer.
Henry evangelizes and teaches with international
prophetic leaders in 10 countries.

His testimony of his former occult leadership experiences of seven generations has enabled him to share the love of God and his delivering power.

Charisma magazine shared is testimony in 2000. 750,000 Hindus translated the article in their language and accepted Christ.

Dr. Lewis attended several colleges which led to obtain three Doctorates in Counseling, Theology and Christian Education.

Henry and his wife have established churches in the US. Their first church was by the assistance of Aimee Semple McPherson's son, Rolf McPherson, who believed in their calling. Later, Dr. Roy Hicks, Sr. (friend who worked at Angelius Temple with Rolf McPhearson) supported them as well.

Henry and Patricia's spiritual foundation was formed from: Dr. Leonard Heroo (Apostle and President of Zion Bible Institute), McPherson), Evangelist Robert Schambach, Prophet David Wilkerson and Derek Prince, Lester Sumrall etc.

Henry's passionate thirst for the knowledge and truth of God's word led him to obtain a deep relational experience with his Lord and Savior, Jesus Christ – and not a religion – so he could hear and know the voice of God.

His vision is to teach and train a courageous generation the incorruptible Word of God and introduce the power of the Holy Spirit. Henry and Patricia's goal is to bring restoration to all nations including the Native Americans. His wife, Patricia is of the Iroquois nation.

Henry & Patricia coordinated large transformation events in New England under the 'Vision for New England" network which began in Salem, Ma with the help of Rev Ken Steigler & local pastors. Daystar programming promoted the events for 2 years. A transformation video was edited that shares the signs and wonders and miracles that occurred.

Dr. Henry Lewis is ordained with the Assemblies of God.
Henry is also ordained Rabbi through Asher Intrater from the Revive Israel Ministries

He is available for speaking.

FOR MORE INFORMATION

H.A.Lewis
Joshua International

P.O. Box 1799
Maricopa, AZ 85139

Email: Info@halewis.org
Email: Info@ joshua-edu.org

To order or inquire of additional products, visit
us online

Website: www.halewis.org
Visit us on face book

Book Cover Artist: Debbie Wheat
Contact: izayu54@yahoo.com

Book Co-coordinators

Grace Miller
Patricia Lewis

BOOKS

A Quest for Spiritual Power - Redeemed
from the Curse - testimonial
Choisi Par Le Maitre: En quête de puissance
spirituelle - French translation
A Quest for Spiritual Power - Arabic
translation
Nimrod - How religions began and how it
applies today
Spiritual Opposition to the Five Fold
Ministry
The Secret Names of the Strongmen - study
material & prayer manual
Jezebel - human or the spirit of baal?
The Dispensation of the Lion and the lamb
The Return of the Days of Noah

Available on Amazon

www.ingramcontent.com/pod-product-compliance
Lightning Source LLC
Chambersburg PA
CBHW061731020426
42331CB00006B/1197